JOURNAL

MADE IN U.S.A.

Published by F M
ISBN: 978-1-9746452-7-5

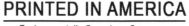

PRINTED IN AMERICA

Environmentally Conscious Company

E.C.C.

Need some help getting started?
We have provided an example on the last page to
help you get started.

"Keep busy and aim to make someone else happy and you might find you get some happiness as a side effect."

Tim Minchin

DATE:__/__/20__

Today I am thankful for...

_____

_____

_____

What would make today amazing?

_____

_____

_____

Affirmations. I am...

_____

_____

_____

Amazing things that happened today...

_____

_____

_____

How could I have made today better for myself and/or someone else?

_____

_____

_____

What am I looking forward to tomorrow?

_____

_____

"MEDIOCRITY WILL ALWAYS TRY TO DRAG EXCELLENCE DOWN TO ITS LEVEL. DON'T TRADE YOUR SUPERIORITY FOR THEIR INFERIORITY."

DATE:__/__/20__

Today I am thankful for...

_____

_____

_____

What would make today amazing?

_____

_____

_____

Affirmations. I am...

_____

_____

_____

Amazing things that happened today...

_____

_____

_____

How could I have made today better for myself and/or someone else?

_____

_____

_____

What am I looking forward to tomorrow?

_____

_____

DATE:__/__/20__

Today I am thankful for...

_____
_____
_____
_____

What would make today amazing?

_____
_____
_____

Affirmations. I am...

_____
_____
_____

Amazing things that happened today...

_____
_____
_____

How could I have made today better for myself and/or someone else?

_____
_____
_____

What am I looking forward to tomorrow?

_____
_____
_____

Today I am thankful for...

_____

_____

_____

What would make today amazing?

_____

_____

_____

Affirmations. I am...

_____

_____

_____

Amazing things that happened today...

_____

_____

How could I have made today better for myself and/or someone else?

_____

_____

_____

What am I looking forward to tomorrow?

_____

_____

DATE:__/__/20__

Today I am thankful for...

_____

_____

_____

What would make today amazing?

_____

_____

_____

Affirmations. I am...

_____

_____

_____

Amazing things that happened today...

_____

_____

_____

How could I have made today better for myself and/or someone else?

_____

_____

_____

What am I looking forward to tomorrow?

_____

_____

_____

Today I am thankful for...

_____

_____

_____

What would make today amazing?

_____

_____

_____

Affirmations. I am...

_____

_____

_____

Amazing things that happened today...

_____

_____

_____

How could I have made today better for myself and/or someone else?

_____

_____

_____

What am I looking forward to tomorrow?

_____

_____

_____

"Happiness is a habit – cultivate it."
Elbert Hubbard

Date:__/__/20__

Today I am thankful for...

_____

_____

_____

What would make today amazing?

_____

_____

_____

Affirmations. I am...

_____

_____

_____

Amazing things that happened today...

_____

_____

_____

How could I have made today better for myself and/or someone else?

_____

_____

What am I looking forward to tomorrow?

_____

_____

DATE:__/__/20__

Today I am thankful for...

_____
_____
_____

What would make today amazing?

_____
_____
_____

Affirmations. I am...

_____
_____
_____

Amazing things that happened today...

_____
_____
_____

How could I have made today better for myself and/or someone else?

_____
_____
_____

What am I looking forward to tomorrow?

_____
_____
_____

DATE:__/__/20__

Today I am thankful for...

_____

_____

_____

What would make today amazing?

_____

_____

_____

Affirmations. I am...

_____

_____

_____

Amazing things that happened today...

_____

_____

How could I have made today better for myself and/or someone else?

_____

_____

_____

What am I looking forward to tomorrow?

_____

_____

"UNTIL YOU MAKE PEACE WITH WHO YOU ARE, YOU'LL NEVER BE CONTENT WITH WHAT YOU HAVE." DORIS MORTMAN

DATE:__/__/20__

Today I am thankful for...

_____
_____
_____

What would make today amazing?

_____
_____
_____

Affirmations. I am...

_____
_____
_____

Amazing things that happened today...

_____
_____

How could I have made today better for myself and/or someone else?

_____
_____
_____

What am I looking forward to tomorrow?

_____
_____
_____

"THOSE WHO ARE THE HAPPIEST, NEVER DID HAVE EVERYTHING. BUT RATHER, THEY ARE THANKFUL FOR WHAT THEY HAVE."

DATE:__/__/20__

Today I am thankful for...

_____

_____

_____

What would make today amazing?

_____

_____

_____

Affirmations. I am...

_____

_____

_____

Amazing things that happened today...

_____

_____

_____

How could I have made today better for myself and/or someone else?

_____

_____

What am I looking forward to tomorrow?

_____

_____

"IF YOU WANT HAPPINESS FOR AN HOUR – TAKE A NAP. IF YOU WANT HAPPINESS FOR A DAY – GO FISHING. IF YOU WANT, HAPPINESS FOR A YEAR – INHERIT A FORTUNE. IF YOU WANT HAPPINESS FOR A LIFETIME – HELP SOMEONE ELSE."

DATE:__/__/20__

Today I am thankful for...

_____

_____

_____

What would make today amazing?

_____

_____

_____

Affirmations. I am...

_____

_____

_____

Amazing things that happened today...

_____

_____

_____

How could I have made today better for myself and/or someone else?

_____

_____

_____

What am I looking forward to tomorrow?

_____

_____

_____

"PEOPLE WILL FORGET WHAT YOU SAID, PEOPLE
WILL FORGET WHAT YOU DID, BUT THEY WILL
NEVER FORGET HOW YOU MADE THEM FEEL.."

DATE:__/__/20__

Today I am thankful for...

_____
_____
_____

What would make today amazing?

_____
_____
_____

Affirmations. I am...

_____
_____
_____

Amazing things that happened today...

_____
_____
_____

How could I have made today better for myself and/or someone else?

_____
_____
_____

What am I looking forward to tomorrow?

_____
_____
_____

Today I am thankful for...

_____
_____
_____

What would make today amazing?

_____
_____
_____

Affirmations. I am...

_____
_____
_____

Amazing things that happened today...

_____
_____
_____

How could I have made today better for myself and/or someone else?

_____
_____
_____

What am I looking forward to tomorrow?

_____
_____

DATE:__/__/20__

Today I am thankful for...

_____

_____

_____

What would make today amazing?

_____

_____

Affirmations. I am...

_____

_____

_____

Amazing things that happened today...

_____

_____

_____

How could I have made today better for myself and/or someone else?

_____

_____

_____

What am I looking forward to tomorrow?

_____

_____

_____

Today I am thankful for...

_____
_____
_____

What would make today amazing?

_____
_____
_____

Affirmations. I am...

_____
_____
_____

Amazing things that happened today...

_____
_____
_____

How could I have made today better for myself and/or someone else?

_____
_____
_____

What am I looking forward to tomorrow?

_____
_____

DATE:__/__/20__

Today I am thankful for...

_____

_____

_____

What would make today amazing?

_____

_____

_____

Affirmations. I am...

_____

_____

_____

Amazing things that happened today...

_____

_____

_____

How could I have made today better for myself and/or someone else?

_____

_____

_____

What am I looking forward to tomorrow?

_____

_____

_____

"No one saves us but ourselves. No one can and no one may. We ourselves must walk the path." Gautama Buddha

Date:__/__/20__

Today I am thankful for...

_____

_____

_____

What would make today amazing?

_____

_____

_____

Affirmations. I am...

_____

_____

_____

Amazing things that happened today...

_____

_____

_____

How could I have made today better for myself and/or someone else?

_____

_____

_____

What am I looking forward to tomorrow?

_____

_____

"NO ONE CAN ESCAPE DEATH AND UNHAPPINESS.
IF PEOPLE EXPECT ONLY HAPPINESS IN LIFE,
THEY WILL BE DISAPPOINTED."
GAUTAMA BUDDHA

DATE:__/__/20__

Today I am thankful for...

What would make today amazing?

Affirmations. I am...

Amazing things that happened today...

How could I have made today better for myself and/or someone else?

What am I looking forward to tomorrow?

"IT IS BETTER TO TRAVEL WELL THAN TO
ARRIVE." » GAUTAMA BUDDHA

DATE:__/__/20__

Today I am thankful for...

What would make today amazing?

Affirmations. I am...

Amazing things that happened today...

How could I have made today better for myself and/or someone else?

What am I looking forward to tomorrow?

"NO ONE CAN ESCAPE DEATH AND UNHAPPINESS.
IF PEOPLE EXPECT ONLY HAPPINESS IN LIFE,
THEY WILL BE DISAPPOINTED."
GAUTAMA BUDDHA

DATE:__/__/20__

Today I am thankful for...

___

___

___

What would make today amazing?

___

___

___

Affirmations. I am...

___

___

___

Amazing things that happened today...

___

___

___

How could I have made today better for myself and/or someone else?

___

___

___

What am I looking forward to tomorrow?

___

___

"WE ARE FORMED AND MOLDED BY OUR THOUGHTS. THOSE WHOSE MINDS ARE SHAPED BY SELFLESS THOUGHTS GIVE JOY WHEN THEY SPEAK OR ACT. JOY FOLLOWS THEM LIKE A "

DATE:__/__/20__

Today I am thankful for...

_____

_____

_____

What would make today amazing?

_____

_____

_____

Affirmations. I am...

_____

_____

_____

Amazing things that happened today...

_____

_____

_____

How could I have made today better for myself and/or someone else?

_____

_____

_____

What am I looking forward to tomorrow?

_____

_____

_____

"WORK OUT YOUR OWN SALVATION. DO NOT DEPEND ON OTHERS." GAUTAMA BUDDHA

DATE:__/__/20__

Today I am thankful for...

What would make today amazing?

Affirmations. I am...

Amazing things that happened today...

How could I have made today better for myself and/or someone else?

What am I looking forward to tomorrow?

"GIVE ME SIX HOURS TO CHOP DOWN A TREE,
AND I WILL SPEND THE FIRST FOUR SHARPENING
THE AXE." AB LINCOLN

DATE:__/__/20__

Today I am thankful for...

What would make today amazing?

Affirmations. I am...

Amazing things that happened today...

How could I have made today better for myself and/or someone else?

What am I looking forward to tomorrow?

DATE:__/__/20__

Today I am thankful for...

_____

_____

_____

What would make today amazing?

_____

_____

_____

Affirmations. I am...

_____

_____

_____

Amazing things that happened today...

_____

_____

_____

How could I have made today better for myself and/or someone else?

_____

_____

_____

What am I looking forward to tomorrow?

_____

_____

_____

"MOST FOLKS ARE AS HAPPY AS THEY MAKE UP
THEIR MINDS TO BE."
AB LINCOLN

DATE:__/__/20__

Today I am thankful for...

_____
_____
_____

What would make today amazing?

_____
_____
_____

Affirmations. I am...

_____
_____
_____

Amazing things that happened today...

_____
_____

How could I have made today better for myself and/or someone else?

_____
_____
_____

What am I looking forward to tomorrow?

_____
_____

DATE:__/__/20__

Today I am thankful for...

What would make today amazing?

Affirmations. I am...

Amazing things that happened today...

How could I have made today better for myself and/or someone else?

What am I looking forward to tomorrow?

DATE:__/__/20__

Today I am thankful for...

_____

_____

_____

What would make today amazing?

_____

_____

_____

Affirmations. I am...

_____

_____

_____

Amazing things that happened today...

_____

_____

_____

How could I have made today better for myself and/or someone else?

_____

_____

_____

What am I looking forward to tomorrow?

_____

_____

_____

"I WALK SLOWLY, BUT I NEVER WALK BACKWARD." AB LINCOLN

DATE:__/__/20__

Today I am thankful for...

_____

_____

_____

What would make today amazing?

_____

_____

_____

Affirmations. I am...

_____

_____

_____

Amazing things that happened today...

_____

_____

_____

How could I have made today better for myself and/or someone else?

_____

_____

_____

What am I looking forward to tomorrow?

_____

_____

_____

"IN TEACHING OTHERS WE TEACH OURSELVES."

DATE:__/__/20__

Today I am thankful for...

_____
_____
_____

What would make today amazing?

_____
_____
_____

Affirmations. I am...

_____
_____
_____

Amazing things that happened today...

_____
_____

How could I have made today better for myself and/or someone else?

_____
_____
_____

What am I looking forward to tomorrow?

_____
_____

DATE:__/__/20__

Today I am thankful for...

_____

_____

_____

What would make today amazing?

_____

_____

_____

Affirmations. I am...

_____

_____

_____

Amazing things that happened today...

_____

_____

_____

How could I have made today better for myself and/or someone else?

_____

_____

What am I looking forward to tomorrow?

_____

_____

_____

DATE:__/__/20__

Today I am thankful for...

_____
_____
_____

What would make today amazing?

_____
_____
_____

Affirmations. I am...

_____
_____
_____

Amazing things that happened today...

_____
_____
_____

How could I have made today better for myself and/or someone else?

_____
_____
_____

What am I looking forward to tomorrow?

_____
_____

Today I am thankful for...

_____
_____
_____

What would make today amazing?

_____
_____
_____

Affirmations. I am...

_____
_____
_____

Amazing things that happened today...

_____
_____
_____

How could I have made today better for myself and/or someone else?

_____
_____
_____

What am I looking forward to tomorrow?

_____
_____

DATE:__/__/20__

Today I am thankful for...

What would make today amazing?

Affirmations. I am...

Amazing things that happened today...

How could I have made today better for myself and/or someone else?

What am I looking forward to tomorrow?

"IF YOU HAVE NEVER FAILED YOU HAVE NEVER LIVED."

DATE:__/__/20__

Today I am thankful for...

What would make today amazing?

Affirmations. I am...

Amazing things that happened today...

How could I have made today better for myself and/or someone else?

What am I looking forward to tomorrow?

Today I am thankful for...

_____

_____

_____

What would make today amazing?

_____

_____

_____

Affirmations. I am...

_____

_____

_____

Amazing things that happened today...

_____

_____

_____

How could I have made today better for myself and/or someone else?

_____

_____

_____

What am I looking forward to tomorrow?

_____

_____

_____

Today I am thankful for...

_____
_____
_____

What would make today amazing?

_____
_____
_____

Affirmations. I am...

_____
_____
_____

Amazing things that happened today...

_____
_____
_____

How could I have made today better for myself and/or someone else?

_____
_____
_____

What am I looking forward to tomorrow?

_____
_____
_____

Today I am thankful for...

_____

_____

_____

What would make today amazing?

_____

_____

_____

Affirmations. I am...

_____

_____

_____

Amazing things that happened today...

_____

_____

How could I have made today better for myself and/or someone else?

_____

_____

_____

What am I looking forward to tomorrow?

_____

_____

_____

"WE BECOME WHAT WE THINK ABOUT."
EARL NIGHTINGALE

DATE:__/__/20__

Today I am thankful for...

_____

_____

_____

What would make today amazing?

_____

_____

_____

Affirmations. I am...

_____

_____

_____

Amazing things that happened today...

_____

_____

_____

How could I have made today better for myself and/or someone else?

_____

_____

_____

What am I looking forward to tomorrow?

_____

_____

_____

"An obstacle is often a stepping stone."
PRESCOTT BUSH

DATE:__/__/20__

Today I am thankful for...

_____
_____
_____

What would make today amazing?

_____
_____
_____

Affirmations. I am...

_____
_____
_____

Amazing things that happened today...

_____
_____
_____

How could I have made today better for myself and/or someone else?

_____
_____
_____

What am I looking forward to tomorrow?

_____
_____

"ACTION IS THE FOUNDATIONAL KEY TO ALL
SUCCESS." PABLO PICASSO

DATE:__/__/20__

Today I am thankful for...

_____

_____

_____

What would make today amazing?

_____

_____

_____

Affirmations. I am...

_____

_____

_____

Amazing things that happened today...

_____

_____

_____

How could I have made today better for myself and/or someone else?

_____

_____

_____

What am I looking forward to tomorrow?

_____

_____

_____

Date:__/__/20__

Today I am thankful for...

_____

_____

_____

What would make today amazing?

_____

_____

_____

Affirmations. I am...

_____

_____

_____

Amazing things that happened today...

_____

_____

_____

How could I have made today better for myself and/or someone else?

_____

_____

_____

What am I looking forward to tomorrow?

_____

_____

_____

"HOPE IS THE HEARTBEAT OF THE SOUL.."
MICHELLE HORST

DATE:__/__/20__

Today I am thankful for...

_____
_____
_____

What would make today amazing?

_____
_____
_____

Affirmations. I am...

_____
_____
_____

Amazing things that happened today...

_____
_____
_____

How could I have made today better for myself and/or someone else?

_____
_____
_____

What am I looking forward to tomorrow?

_____
_____

"THE OBSTACLE IS THE PATH."

DATE:__/__/20__

Today I am thankful for...

_____
_____
_____

What would make today amazing?

_____
_____
_____

Affirmations. I am...

_____
_____
_____

Amazing things that happened today...

_____
_____
_____

How could I have made today better for myself and/or someone else?

_____
_____
_____

What am I looking forward to tomorrow?

_____
_____

"DO ONE THING EVERY DAY THAT SCARES YOU."
ELEANOR ROOSEVELT

DATE:__/__/20__

Today I am thankful for...

_____

_____

_____

What would make today amazing?

_____

_____

_____

Affirmations. I am...

_____

_____

_____

Amazing things that happened today...

_____

_____

_____

How could I have made today better for myself and/or someone else?

_____

_____

_____

What am I looking forward to tomorrow?

_____

_____

_____

"Do not confine your children to your own learning, for they were born in another time."

Date:__/__/20__

Today I am thankful for...

_____

_____

_____

What would make today amazing?

_____

_____

_____

Affirmations. I am...

_____

_____

_____

Amazing things that happened today...

_____

_____

_____

How could I have made today better for myself and/or someone else?

_____

_____

_____

What am I looking forward to tomorrow?

_____

_____

Today I am thankful for...

What would make today amazing?

Affirmations. I am...

Amazing things that happened today...

How could I have made today better for myself and/or someone else?

What am I looking forward to tomorrow?

DATE:__/__/20__

Today I am thankful for...

_____

_____

_____

What would make today amazing?

_____

_____

_____

Affirmations. I am...

_____

_____

_____

Amazing things that happened today...

_____

_____

_____

How could I have made today better for myself and/or someone else?

_____

_____

_____

What am I looking forward to tomorrow?

_____

_____

"ALL OUR WORDS FROM LOOSE USING HAVE LOST THEIR EDGE."
ERNEST HEMINGWAY

DATE:__/__/20__

Today I am thankful for...

_____
_____
_____

What would make today amazing?

_____
_____

Affirmations. I am...

_____
_____

Amazing things that happened today...

_____
_____

How could I have made today better for myself and/or someone else?

_____
_____

What am I looking forward to tomorrow?

_____
_____

Today I am thankful for...

What would make today amazing?

Affirmations. I am...

Amazing things that happened today...

How could I have made today better for myself and/or someone else?

What am I looking forward to tomorrow?

DATE:__/__/20__

Today I am thankful for...

_____

_____

_____

What would make today amazing?

_____

_____

_____

Affirmations. I am...

_____

_____

_____

Amazing things that happened today...

_____

_____

_____

How could I have made today better for myself and/or someone else?

_____

_____

_____

What am I looking forward to tomorrow?

_____

_____

_____

Today I am thankful for...

_____

_____

_____

What would make today amazing?

_____

_____

_____

Affirmations. I am...

_____

_____

_____

Amazing things that happened today...

_____

_____

_____

How could I have made today better for myself and/or someone else?

_____

_____

_____

What am I looking forward to tomorrow?

_____

_____

_____

DATE:__/__/20__

Today I am thankful for...

_____

_____

_____

What would make today amazing?

_____

_____

_____

Affirmations. I am...

_____

_____

_____

Amazing things that happened today...

_____

_____

How could I have made today better for myself and/or someone else?

_____

_____

What am I looking forward to tomorrow?

_____

_____

"YOU MUST DO THE THING WHICH YOU THINK
YOU CANNOT DO." -ELEANOR ROOSEVELT

DATE:__/__/20__

Today I am thankful for...

_____

_____

_____

What would make today amazing?

_____

_____

_____

Affirmations. I am...

_____

_____

_____

Amazing things that happened today...

_____

_____

_____

How could I have made today better for myself and/or someone else?

_____

_____

_____

What am I looking forward to tomorrow?

_____

_____

"DO SOMETHING NOW THAT WILL MAKE THE
PERSON YOU'LL BE TOMORROW PROUD TO HAVE
BEEN THE PERSON YOU ARE TODAY"

DATE:__/__/20__

Today I am thankful for...

What would make today amazing?

Affirmations. I am...

Amazing things that happened today...

How could I have made today better for myself and/or someone else?

What am I looking forward to tomorrow?

"MEDIOCRITY WILL ALWAYS TRY TO DRAG
EXCELLENCE DOWN TO ITS LEVEL. DON'T TRADE
YOUR SUPERIORITY FOR THEIR INFERIORITY."

DATE:__/__/20__

Today I am thankful for...

What would make today amazing?

Affirmations. I am...

Amazing things that happened today...

How could I have made today better for myself and/or someone else?

What am I looking forward to tomorrow?

"ALL MEN DESIRE PEACE, BUT VERY FEW DESIRE
THE THINGS THAT MAKE PEACE."

DATE:__/__/20__

Today I am thankful for...

What would make today amazing?

Affirmations. I am...

Amazing things that happened today...

How could I have made today better for myself and/or someone else?

What am I looking forward to tomorrow?

"IN ORDER TO CARRY A POSITIVE ACTION WE
MUST FIRST DEVELOP A POSITIVE VISION."
DALAI LAMA

DATE:__/__/20__

Today I am thankful for...

What would make today amazing?

Affirmations. I am...

Amazing things that happened today...

How could I have made today better for myself and/or someone else?

What am I looking forward to tomorrow?

DATE:__/__/20__

Today I am thankful for...

What would make today amazing?

Affirmations. I am...

Amazing things that happened today...

How could I have made today better for myself and/or someone else?

What am I looking forward to tomorrow?

Today I am thankful for...

_____

_____

_____

What would make today amazing?

_____

_____

_____

Affirmations. I am...

_____

_____

_____

Amazing things that happened today...

_____

_____

_____

How could I have made today better for myself and/or someone else?

_____

_____

_____

What am I looking forward to tomorrow?

_____

_____

"ACT THE WAY YOU WANT TO FEEL."
GRETCHEN RUBIN

DATE:__/__/20__

Today I am thankful for...

_____
_____
_____

What would make today amazing?

_____
_____
_____

Affirmations. I am...

_____
_____
_____

Amazing things that happened today...

_____
_____
_____

How could I have made today better for myself and/or someone else?

_____
_____

What am I looking forward to tomorrow?

_____
_____

DATE:__/__/20__

Today I am thankful for...

_____
_____
_____

What would make today amazing?

_____
_____
_____

Affirmations. I am...

_____
_____
_____

Amazing things that happened today...

_____
_____
_____

How could I have made today better for myself and/or someone else?

_____
_____
_____

What am I looking forward to tomorrow?

_____
_____

DATE:__/__/20__

Today I am thankful for...

_____

_____

_____

What would make today amazing?

_____

_____

_____

Affirmations. I am...

_____

_____

_____

Amazing things that happened today...

_____

_____

_____

How could I have made today better for myself and/or someone else?

_____

_____

_____

What am I looking forward to tomorrow?

_____

_____

_____

Today I am thankful for...

_____

_____

_____

What would make today amazing?

_____

_____

_____

Affirmations. I am...

_____

_____

_____

Amazing things that happened today...

_____

_____

_____

How could I have made today better for myself and/or someone else?

_____

_____

_____

What am I looking forward to tomorrow?

_____

_____

Today I am thankful for...

_____
_____
_____

What would make today amazing?

_____
_____
_____

Affirmations. I am...

_____
_____
_____

Amazing things that happened today...

_____
_____
_____

How could I have made today better for myself and/or someone else?

_____
_____
_____

What am I looking forward to tomorrow?

_____
_____

"THOSE WHO ARE THE HAPPIEST, NEVER DID HAVE EVERYTHING. BUT RATHER, THEY ARE THANKFUL FOR WHAT THEY HAVE."

DATE:__/__/20__

Today I am thankful for...

_____

_____

_____

What would make today amazing?

_____

_____

_____

Affirmations. I am...

_____

_____

_____

Amazing things that happened today...

_____

_____

_____

How could I have made today better for myself and/or someone else?

_____

_____

_____

What am I looking forward to tomorrow?

_____

_____

"PEOPLE WILL FORGET WHAT YOU SAID, PEOPLE WILL FORGET WHAT YOU DID, BUT THEY WILL NEVER FORGET HOW YOU MADE THEM FEEL.."

DATE:__/__/20__

Today I am thankful for...

What would make today amazing?

Affirmations. I am...

Amazing things that happened today...

How could I have made today better for myself and/or someone else?

What am I looking forward to tomorrow?

DATE:__/__/20__

Today I am thankful for...

_____

_____

_____

What would make today amazing?

_____

_____

_____

Affirmations. I am...

_____

_____

_____

Amazing things that happened today...

_____

_____

_____

How could I have made today better for myself and/or someone else?

_____

_____

_____

What am I looking forward to tomorrow?

_____

_____

"IT IS BETTER TO TRAVEL WELL THAN TO ARRIVE." » GAUTAMA BUDDHA

DATE:__/__/20__

Today I am thankful for...

_____

_____

_____

What would make today amazing?

_____

_____

_____

Affirmations. I am...

_____

_____

_____

Amazing things that happened today...

_____

_____

How could I have made today better for myself and/or someone else?

_____

_____

_____

What am I looking forward to tomorrow?

_____

_____

_____

"NO ONE SAVES US BUT OURSELVES. NO ONE CAN AND NO ONE MAY. WE OURSELVES MUST WALK THE PATH." GAUTAMA BUDDHA

DATE:__/__/20__

Today I am thankful for...

_____
_____
_____

What would make today amazing?

_____
_____
_____

Affirmations. I am...

_____
_____
_____

Amazing things that happened today...

_____
_____
_____

How could I have made today better for myself and/or someone else?

_____
_____
_____

What am I looking forward to tomorrow?

_____
_____
_____

"FILL THE BRAIN WITH HIGH THOUGHTS, HIGHEST IDEALS PLACE THEM DAY AND NIGHT BEFORE YOU AND OUT OF THAT WILL COME GREAT WORK."

DATE:__/__/20__

Today I am thankful for...

What would make today amazing?

Affirmations. I am...

Amazing things that happened today...

How could I have made today better for myself and/or someone else?

What am I looking forward to tomorrow?

"As different streams having different sources all mingle their waters in the sea, so different tendencies, various though they appear, crooked or straight, all lead to God." Swami Vivekananda

Date:__/__/20__

Today I am thankful for...

_____
_____
_____

What would make today amazing?

_____
_____
_____

Affirmations. I am...

_____
_____
_____

Amazing things that happened today...

_____
_____
_____

How could I have made today better for myself and/or someone else?

_____
_____
_____

What am I looking forward to tomorrow?

_____
_____

DATE:__/__/20__

Today I am thankful for...

___

___

___

What would make today amazing?

___

___

___

Affirmations. I am...

___

___

___

Amazing things that happened today...

___

___

___

How could I have made today better for myself and/or someone else?

___

___

___

What am I looking forward to tomorrow?

___

___

___

"YOU CANNOT BELIEVE IN GOD UNTIL YOU
BELIEVE IN YOURSELF."

DATE:__/__/20__

Today I am thankful for...

_____
_____
_____

What would make today amazing?

_____
_____
_____

Affirmations. I am...

_____
_____
_____

Amazing things that happened today...

_____
_____
_____

How could I have made today better for myself and/or someone else?

_____
_____
_____

What am I looking forward to tomorrow?

_____
_____
_____

"YOU HAVE TO GROW FROM THE INSIDE OUT.
NONE CAN TEACH YOU, NONE CAN MAKE YOU
SPIRITUAL. THERE IS NO OTHER TEACHER BUT
YOUR OWN SOUL."

DATE:__/__/20__

Today I am thankful for...

What would make today amazing?

Affirmations. I am...

Amazing things that happened today...

How could I have made today better for myself and/or someone else?

What am I looking forward to tomorrow?

"AS DIFFERENT STREAMS HAVING DIFFERENT
SOURCES ALL MINGLE THEIR WATERS IN THE SEA,
SO DIFFERENT TENDENCIES, VARIOUS THOUGH
THEY APPEAR, CROOKED OR STRAIGHT, ALL LEAD
TO GOD." SWAMI VIVEKANANDA

DATE:__/__/20__

Today I am thankful for...

What would make today amazing?

Affirmations. I am...

Amazing things that happened today...

How could I have made today better for myself and/or someone else?

What am I looking forward to tomorrow?

"FILL THE BRAIN WITH HIGH THOUGHTS,
HIGHEST IDEALS PLACE THEM DAY AND NIGHT
BEFORE YOU AND OUT OF THAT WILL COME
GREAT WORK."

DATE:__/__/20__

Today I am thankful for...

What would make today amazing?

Affirmations. I am...

Amazing things that happened today...

How could I have made today better for myself and/or someone else?

What am I looking forward to tomorrow?

"BY THE STUDY OF DIFFERENT RELIGIONS WE FIND THAT IN ESSENCE THEY ARE ONE."

DATE:__/__/20__

Today I am thankful for...

_____
_____
_____

What would make today amazing?

_____
_____
_____

Affirmations. I am...

_____
_____
_____

Amazing things that happened today...

_____
_____
_____

How could I have made today better for myself and/or someone else?

_____
_____
_____

What am I looking forward to tomorrow?

_____
_____

THE WORLD IS BEAUTIFUL OUTSIDE WHEN
THERE IS STABILITY INSIDE.

DATE:__/__/20__

Today I am thankful for...

What would make today amazing?

Affirmations. I am...

Amazing things that happened today...

How could I have made today better for myself and/or someone else?

What am I looking forward to tomorrow?

YOUR JOURNEY WILL BE MUCH LIGHTER AND EASIER IF YOU DON'T CARRY YOUR PAST WITH YOU.

DATE:__/__/20_

Today I am thankful for...

_____
_____
_____

What would make today amazing?

_____
_____
_____

Affirmations. I am...

_____
_____

Amazing things that happened today...

_____
_____
_____

How could I have made today better for myself and/or someone else?

_____
_____
_____

What am I looking forward to tomorrow?

_____
_____

DATE:__/__/20__

Today I am thankful for...

_____

_____

_____

What would make today amazing?

_____

_____

_____

Affirmations. I am...

_____

_____

_____

Amazing things that happened today...

_____

_____

_____

How could I have made today better for myself and/or someone else?

_____

_____

_____

What am I looking forward to tomorrow?

_____

_____

MORNING IS AN IMPORTANT TIME OF DAY,
BECAUSE HOW YOU SPEND YOUR MORNING CAN
OFTEN TELL YOU WHAT KIND OF DAY YOU ARE
GOING TO HAVE. LEMONY SNICKET

DATE:__/__/20__

Today I am thankful for...

___

___

___

What would make today amazing?

___

___

___

Affirmations. I am...

___

___

___

Amazing things that happened today...

___

___

___

How could I have made today better for myself and/or someone else?

___

___

___

What am I looking forward to tomorrow?

___

___

THE SUN HAS NOT CAUGHT ME IN BED IN FIFTY
YEARS. THOMAS JEFFERSON

DATE:__/__/20__

Today I am thankful for...

_____

_____

_____

What would make today amazing?

_____

_____

_____

Affirmations. I am...

_____

_____

_____

Amazing things that happened today...

_____

_____

_____

How could I have made today better for myself and/or someone else?

_____

_____

_____

What am I looking forward to tomorrow?

_____

_____

Today I am thankful for...

_____
_____
_____

What would make today amazing?

_____
_____
_____

Affirmations. I am...

_____
_____
_____

Amazing things that happened today...

_____
_____
_____

How could I have made today better for myself and/or someone else?

_____
_____
_____

What am I looking forward to tomorrow?

_____
_____

EVEN AFTER ALL THIS TIME, THE SUN NEVER
SAYS TO THE EARTH. "YOU OWE ME."

DATE:__/__/20__

Today I am thankful for...

_____

_____

_____

What would make today amazing?

_____

_____

_____

Affirmations. I am...

_____

_____

_____

Amazing things that happened today...

_____

_____

_____

How could I have made today better for myself and/or someone else?

_____

_____

_____

What am I looking forward to tomorrow?

_____

_____

_____

THERE IS NO SNOOZE BUTTON ON A CAT WHO
WANTS BREAKFAST.

DATE:__/__/20__

Today I am thankful for...

_____

_____

_____

What would make today amazing?

_____

_____

_____

Affirmations. I am...

_____

_____

_____

Amazing things that happened today...

_____

_____

_____

How could I have made today better for myself and/or someone else?

_____

_____

_____

What am I looking forward to tomorrow?

_____

_____

BE WILLING TO BE A BEGINNER EVERY SINGLE
MORNING. MEISTER ECKHART

DATE:__/__/20__

Today I am thankful for...

What would make today amazing?

Affirmations. I am...

Amazing things that happened today...

How could I have made today better for myself and/or someone else?

What am I looking forward to tomorrow?

NOW THAT YOUR EYES ARE OPEN, MAKE THE SUN
JEALOUS WITH YOUR BURNING PASSION TO START
THE DAY. MAKE THE SUN JEALOUS OR STAY IN
BED. MALAK EL HALABI

DATE:__/__/20__

Today I am thankful for...

_____

_____

_____

What would make today amazing?

_____

_____

_____

Affirmations. I am...

_____

_____

_____

Amazing things that happened today...

_____

_____

_____

How could I have made today better for myself and/or someone else?

_____

_____

_____

What am I looking forward to tomorrow?

_____

_____

SMILE IN THE MIRROR. DO THAT EVERY MORNING
AND YOU'LL START TO SEE A BIG DIFFERENCE IN
YOUR LIFE. YOKO ONO

DATE:__/__/20__

Today I am thankful for...

What would make today amazing?

Affirmations. I am...

Amazing things that happened today...

How could I have made today better for myself and/or someone else?

What am I looking forward to tomorrow?

EVERY MORNING IS A BEAUTIFUL MORNING.

DATE:__/__/20_

Today I am thankful for...

_____

_____

_____

What would make today amazing?

_____

_____

_____

Affirmations. I am...

_____

_____

_____

Amazing things that happened today...

_____

_____

_____

How could I have made today better for myself and/or someone else?

_____

_____

_____

What am I looking forward to tomorrow?

_____

_____

ONE KEY TO SUCCESS IS TO HAVE LUNCH AT THE
TIME OF DAY MOST PEOPLE HAVE BREAKFAST.
ROBERT BRAULT

DATE:__/__/20__

Today I am thankful for...

What would make today amazing?

Affirmations. I am...

Amazing things that happened today...

How could I have made today better for myself and/or someone else?

What am I looking forward to tomorrow?

Today I am thankful for...

What would make today amazing?

Affirmations. I am...

Amazing things that happened today...

How could I have made today better for myself and/or someone else?

What am I looking forward to tomorrow?

ONE KEY TO SUCCESS IS TO HAVE LUNCH AT THE
TIME OF DAY MOST PEOPLE HAVE BREAKFAST.
ROBERT BRAULT

DATE:__/__/20__

Today I am thankful for...

What would make today amazing?

Affirmations. I am...

Amazing things that happened today...

How could I have made today better for myself and/or someone else?

What am I looking forward to tomorrow?

OLD FRIENDS PASS AWAY, NEW FRIENDS APPEAR.
IT IS JUST LIKE THE DAYS. AN OLD DAY PASSES, A
NEW DAY ARRIVES. THE IMPORTANT THING IS TO
MAKE IT MEANINGFUL. A MEANINGFUL FRIEND OR
A MEANINGFUL DAY. DALAI

DATE:__/__/20__

Today I am thankful for...

What would make today amazing?

Affirmations. I am...

Amazing things that happened today...

How could I have made today better for myself and/or someone else?

What am I looking forward to tomorrow?

THE SUN IS NEW EACH DAY.
HERACLITUS

DATE:__/__/20__

Today I am thankful for...

What would make today amazing?

Affirmations. I am...

Amazing things that happened today...

How could I have made today better for myself and/or someone else?

What am I looking forward to tomorrow?

DATE:__/__/20__

Today I am thankful for...

_____
_____
_____
_____

What would make today amazing?

_____
_____
_____
_____

Affirmations. I am...

_____
_____
_____

Amazing things that happened today...

_____
_____
_____

How could I have made today better for myself and/or someone else?

_____
_____
_____

What am I looking forward to tomorrow?

_____
_____

DATE:__/__/20__

Today I am thankful for...

_____

_____

_____

What would make today amazing?

_____

_____

_____

Affirmations. I am...

_____

_____

_____

Amazing things that happened today...

_____

_____

_____

How could I have made today better for myself and/or someone else?

_____

_____

_____

What am I looking forward to tomorrow?

_____

_____

I HAVE ALWAYS BEEN DELIGHTED AT THE
PROSPECT OF A NEW DAY, A FRESH TRY, ONE
MORE START, WITH PERHAPS A BIT OF MAGIC
WAITING SOMEWHERE BEHIND THE MORNING.
B. PRIESTLEY

Date:__/__/20__

Today I am thankful for...

_____
_____
_____

What would make today amazing?

_____
_____
_____

Affirmations. I am...

_____
_____
_____

Amazing things that happened today...

_____
_____
_____

How could I have made today better for myself and/or someone else?

_____
_____
_____

What am I looking forward to tomorrow?

_____
_____
_____

DATE:__/__/20__

Today I am thankful for...

What would make today amazing?

Affirmations. I am...

Amazing things that happened today...

How could I have made today better for myself and/or someone else?

What am I looking forward to tomorrow?

LOVE. FALL IN LOVE AND STAY IN LOVE. WRITE
ONLY WHAT YOU LOVE, AND LOVE WHAT YOU
WRITE. THE KEY WORD IS LOVE. YOU HAVE TO
GET UP IN THE MORNING AND WRITE SOMETHING
YOU LOVE, SOMETHING TO LIVE FOR.

DATE:__/__/20__

Today I am thankful for...

_____

_____

_____

What would make today amazing?

_____

_____

_____

Affirmations. I am...

_____

_____

_____

Amazing things that happened today...

_____

_____

_____

How could I have made today better for myself and/or someone else?

_____

_____

_____

What am I looking forward to tomorrow?

_____

_____

_____

EVERY MORNING, I WAKE UP SAYING, I'M STILL
ALIVE, A MIRACLE. AND SO I KEEP ON PUSHING.   DATE:__/__/20__
JIM CARREY

Today I am thankful for...

What would make today amazing?

Affirmations. I am...

Amazing things that happened today...

How could I have made today better for myself and/or someone else?

What am I looking forward to tomorrow?

NOTHING IS MORE BEAUTIFUL THAN THE
LOVELINESS OF THE WOODS BEFORE SUNRISE.
GEORGE WASHINGTON CARVER

DATE:__/__/20__

Today I am thankful for...

_____
_____
_____

What would make today amazing?

_____
_____
_____

Affirmations. I am...

_____
_____
_____

Amazing things that happened today...

_____
_____
_____

How could I have made today better for myself and/or someone else?

_____
_____
_____

What am I looking forward to tomorrow?

_____
_____

THE HAPPINESS OF YOUR LIFE DEPENDS UPON
THE QUALITY OF YOUR THOUGHTS.
SO THINK HAPPY & POSITIVE

DATE:__/__/20__

Today I am thankful for...

What would make today amazing?

Affirmations. I am...

Amazing things that happened today...

How could I have made today better for myself and/or someone else?

What am I looking forward to tomorrow?

DATE:__/__/20__

Today I am thankful for...

_____

_____

_____

What would make today amazing?

_____

_____

_____

Affirmations. I am...

_____

_____

_____

Amazing things that happened today...

_____

_____

_____

How could I have made today better for myself and/or someone else?

_____

_____

_____

What am I looking forward to tomorrow?

_____

_____

WITH THE NEW DAY COMES NEW STRENGTH AND NEW THOUGHTS.

DATE:__/__/20__

Today I am thankful for...

_____

_____

_____

What would make today amazing?

_____

_____

_____

Affirmations. I am...

_____

_____

_____

Amazing things that happened today...

_____

_____

_____

How could I have made today better for myself and/or someone else?

_____

_____

_____

What am I looking forward to tomorrow?

_____

_____

NO MATTER HOW BAD THINGS ARE, YOU CAN AT
LEAST BE HAPPY THAT YOU WOKE UP THIS
MORNING.

D. L HUGHLEY

DATE:__/__/20__

Today I am thankful for...

_____
_____
_____

What would make today amazing?

_____
_____
_____

Affirmations. I am...

_____
_____
_____

Amazing things that happened today...

_____
_____
_____

How could I have made today better for myself and/or someone else?

_____
_____
_____

What am I looking forward to tomorrow?

_____
_____

Today I am thankful for...

_____

_____

_____

What would make today amazing?

_____

_____

_____

Affirmations. I am...

_____

_____

_____

Amazing things that happened today...

_____

_____

_____

How could I have made today better for myself and/or someone else?

_____

_____

_____

What am I looking forward to tomorrow?

_____

_____

_____

Today I am thankful for...

The beautiful sun rise

My amazing math teacher

My amazing little sister

What would make today amazing?

If I have the opportunity to meet someone interesting
at the show tonight.

Affirmations. I am...

I am grateful for my opportunity to be apart of the
soccer team.

Amazing things that happened today...

It was amazing to have someone notice my new glasses.
I passed the test after months of studying!

How could I have made today better for myself and/or someone else?

I really want to volunteer and I think it would be
amazing to help someone less fortunate than me on a
regular schedule.

What am I looking forward to tomorrow?

I am looking forward to eating lunch with Alisha.
I can't wait to see my favorite mentor tomorrow.

11134000R00063

Made in the USA
Lexington, KY
05 October 2018